In memory of Rusty
—Stephanie

❧

For Peggy—artist, friend, and lover of animals
—Liza

I want to thank Ronnie Vostinack, executive director, and Crissandra Van Dyke, shelter manager of Homeward Bound Pets in McMinnville, Oregon. Both took time away from their compassionate work with animals to meet with me and provide valuable feedback on the text. Erin Fettig, volunteer with Oregon Humane Society, and Nancy Carlson, newspaper columnist and dog expert, were critically helpful with their proofreading and commenting. I am indebted to award-winning author and naturalist Ruth A. Musgrave, who generously shared her deep well of knowledge about animals as well as her expertise in nonfiction writing. And, finally, a very special thank-you to my editor at Sleeping Bear Press, Barb McNally, for her guidance and encouragement. —Stephanie

Text Copyright © 2020 Stephanie Shaw
Illustration Copyright © 2020 Liza Woodruff
Design © 2020 Sleeping Bear Press

 SLEEPING BEAR PRESS™

2395 South Huron Parkway, Suite 200,
Ann Arbor, MI 48104
www.sleepingbearpress.com
© Sleeping Bear Press

Printed and bound in the United States.
10 9 8 7 6 5 4 3 2 1

Library of Congress Cataloging-in-Publication Data
Names: Shaw, Stephanie, author. | Woodruff, Liza, illustrator.
Title: Tails from the animal shelter / written by Stephanie Shaw ; illustrated by Liza Woodruff. | Description: Ann Arbor, Michigan : Sleeping Bear Press, [2020] | Audience: Ages 4-8 | Summary: "Poetry and informational text showcase the work of community animal shelters. Ten different fictional animals represent the millions of pets brought to shelters every day. Suggestions on animal adoption, including how to prepare and appropriate pet selection, are included, along with resources list"– Provided by publisher. Identifiers: LCCN 2020006331 | ISBN 9781534110489 (hardcover) | Subjects: LCSH: Animal shelters—Juvenile literature. | Pet adoption—Juvenile literature. | Classification: LCC HV4708 .S545 2020 | DDC 636.08/32–dc23 | LC record available at https://lccn.loc.gov/2020006331

TAILS From the Animal SHELTER

By Stephanie Shaw • Illustrated by Liza Woodruff

Published by Sleeping Bear Press

We're happy to greet you and happy to meet you.
Do you have a hand to lend?
We all need some love and a little care
But mostly we just need a friend.

Every year, about six and a half million pets arrive at community animal shelters throughout the United States. These are known as Humane Societies, shelters, rescue services, or other names that might be specific to a breed of animal. But all face challenges in the numbers of animals in need of help.

Some of the animals are strays; some are rescued from natural disasters or from people who were mistreating them. Some have been given up for adoption because their owners can no longer care for them. The animals you meet in this book represent the millions of pets living in animal shelters everywhere. And these organizations need help in caring for the animals and finding homes for them.

Let's meet them.

Puppy runs to get a cuddle.
Puppy makes a puppy puddle.
Puppy cannot help but piddle.
Happy puppies always dribble.
Older pups have tails that thump
and wiggle from their snout to rump.
As time passes and pups grow,
This little guy won't pee "hello."

Meet Tinkle

There are over three million dogs entering animal shelters nationwide every year! Some are lost and shelters work to find their owners, but most dogs in shelter care are in need of a new home. There are many reasons why dogs come to shelter care. Often it is people problems that cause them to need rehoming. The Shelter Pet Project says people "moving and landlord issues are the top reasons people give up their pets." If you live in a rented home, be sure to check that pets are allowed.

So if you and your family are ready and able to have a pet, the very best place to start is your local animal shelter or rescue organization. If you have an idea of what kind of dog you have your heart set on (size or breed, for example), you can do some research in shelter care and rescue missions to find one.

If you are not sure what type you want, let the shelter work with you to find a good match. With millions of dogs of all ages, sizes, and breeds waiting for their forever homes, you are bound to find just the right one.

Behold my fur! It's long and thick!
I cannot help but give a lick
And keep it tidy, after all—
No shedding! Just one big fur ball.

Meet Hack

Over three million cats enter shelters in the United States every year. Just like dogs, the biggest reason cats are in shelter care is because the owners had to move and the new housing did not allow pets. If you have a home that allows cats, they are great companions. Here are five reasons to adopt a cat:

No need for fencing!
They are happy to live indoors.

No expensive haircuts!
They are neat and groom themselves.

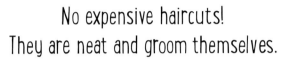

No potty training! They will use a litter box with *almost no training*!

Natural hunters! They will capture house-invading mice.

They exercise themselves! They love to play with you or on their own.

What's black and white and needs a home?
You guessed it. I'm a skunk.
Don't be afraid to take me in.
My stinker is defunct.

Meet Pooter

It's a bit unusual, but some people have pet skunks. If the time comes when they no longer can or want to care for them, pet skunks end up in shelters. These are skunks that have never lived in the wild. They were born in captivity and raised by humans. Pet skunks undergo an operation so they cannot make the very smelly spray they use to defend themselves against predators. Since they cannot defend themselves, pet skunks should never be let loose outdoors. In the wild, they do not know how to behave like a skunk. They wouldn't know how to find food or a place to sleep.

Some states do not allow skunks to be kept as pets. In fact, there are laws in every state about owning wild or exotic animals. If you find a wild animal that is injured or abandoned by its parent, do *not* touch it. Then tell your parents or an adult so they can contact your state wildlife agency for guidance.

This fellow has such great appeal:
No tail, one eye, three legs, one wheel.

Meet Lucky

Sometimes there are animals with health problems, and their owner can no longer take care of them. The loving thing for those owners to do is to ask a shelter to find a home that can provide for the pet's special needs. There are several organizations that only serve animals with different kinds of disabilities. By providing medical care and special equipment such as rear-support leashes or wheelchairs, dogs (and other animals) can live happily for many years! And if you are able, adopting an animal with special needs will bring a grateful and loyal pet into your family.

I am a sweet potbellied pig.
I started small but I grew BIG.
I'm here because of weight I gained,
But I am smart and potty-trained!
I know some tricks. I'm neat and clean.
I'm many things. I'm just not . . .
lean.

Meet Hamlet

It isn't just dogs and cats and small animals that arrive at shelters that need rehoming. Farm animals such as pigs, goats, sheep, and chickens need new homes. There are over two hundred thousand horses alone rescued or surrendered to shelter care every year.

If you are lucky enough to live on a farm and your family can foster or adopt a farm animal, there are many easily found through Humane Society listings in every state. And there are 4-H programs for every type of farm animal imaginable. As a 4-H member, you not only give an animal a new home, but also an opportunity to be shown at county and state fairs.

One exceptional program is Lollypop Farm, Humane Society of Greater Rochester. It has been helping animals since 1873. The farm has programs for rehabilitating and adopting everything from hamsters to horses!

Sssssay there! Could you use a pet
That sssssits and sssstays and doesn't fret
About his fur because he's hairlessss,
Barklesss, beaklesssss, could-not-care-lesssss.
I'd give you sssuch a gentle sssqueeze
If you would jusssst adopt me—*pleassssse?*

Meet Al Dente

Nonpoisonous snakes, lizards, bearded dragons, turtles, and other reptiles are the perfect solution for someone who wants a pet but is allergic to feathers or fur! Reptiles are quiet (no barking), they don't chew on furniture or shoes, and they don't require daily walks or training. With food, fresh water, a clean, comfortable bed, and regular veterinary checkups, they can live a long time. Before searching for a shelter or rescue organization for a reptile pet, check to see what your state's laws are. Hawaii, for example, does not allow ownership of snakes of any kind.

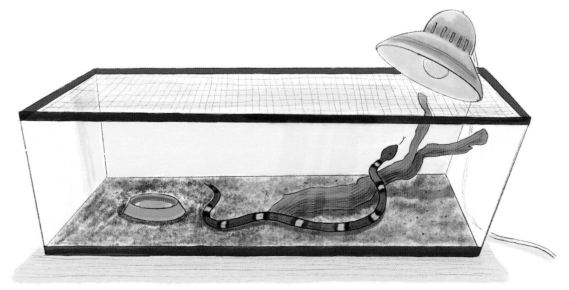

I lived in a magician's hat.
I disappeared and that was that.
Now I'm looking for a bed
That does not rest on someone's head.

Meet Sugar

After dogs and cats, rabbits are the animals most often surrendered to shelters. Most lose their homes because of people problems (owners must move or are no longer willing or able to care for them). Small baby bunnies are often given as gifts. Shelters receive them when they are fully grown. Mature rabbits found in shelter care truly are a great choice for a house pet. Once they have been spayed or neutered, rabbits can be trained to use a litter box. If a home is safety-proofed, they can live indoors just like cats do. If you do not have space for a larger animal, rabbits make a perfect pet. Rabbits live eight to fourteen years, giving lots of family pet enjoyment.

If you need a story,
I can spin you a yarn
Of mousing and hunting
in fields or a barn.
Meet Dickens

I'll sing for my supper!
I'll wear my tuxedo.
You just say the word
and I'm ready to go!
Meet Luciano

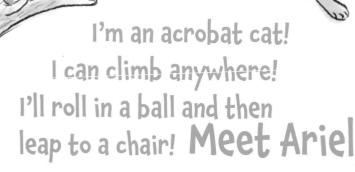

I'm an acrobat cat!
I can climb anywhere!
I'll roll in a ball and then
leap to a chair! **Meet Ariel**

Kitty season is during the warm weather of spring and summer. Shelters and rescue organizations become full when caring for newborn kittens. These little ones are often from mama community cats (cats with no particular home that roam neighborhoods). Kittens abandoned or left at a shelter at birth are vulnerable and need special feeding, warmth, and protection. You might want to think about offering your home to foster a newborn kitten. Within a few weeks under your good care, the kitten will be ready for adoption.

One reason there are so many dogs and cats is because there are just *too many* animals being born. But veterinarians (animal doctors) working with shelters can provide a special operation (*spaying* for female cats and dogs and *neutering* for males). This surgery helps control the overpopulation of animals.

I haven't learned yet how to talk.
My voice is just a high-pitched squawk.
The words I seek are out of reach.
I long for when I do not screech.

Meet Churchill

Like other pets, parrots (including African greys, Amazons, and sulphur-crested cockatoos to name a few) can develop challenging behaviors that might cause them to be placed in a shelter. But there is another reason that is unique to them: they can live a very, very long time—some up to 80 to 100 years! Sometimes their owners grow too old to take care of them.

But bird rescuer Chris Driggins of Vancouver, Washington, developed a great rehoming program just for parrots. Chris matches parrots with military veterans. Parrots for Patriots not only rehomes the birds, but provides companionship to soldiers who need help adjusting to home life after their time of service. Although we do not know how many birds arrive at various rescue organizations or shelters, we do know that in the Pacific Northwest, Chris has matched over 200 parrots with service women and men since the Parrots for Patriots program began in 2015.

Silver muzzle, heart of gold.
Young at heart, very old.

Meet Nana

When thinking about adopting a dog, your first choice may be a puppy. You might have in mind the exact personality you want your puppy to have. But puppies do not stay puppies for very long. As they grow, they not only change in size, but in how they act. One big

advantage of fostering or adopting a senior dog is you know *exactly* the kind of dog they are. Plus, they have a lifetime of experience and generally do not require the extensive training that a puppy does.

Older animals enjoy just being in a safe environment. With no need to be super active, they are often content to be great listeners. All pets deserve to enjoy life even after

they have slowed down. They may be senior animals, but they still have lots of love and companionship to share. Maybe you can provide the "retirement home" they need.

More to Know and How to Help

THE BEGINNING OF SHELTERS

In 1863 American diplomat Henry Bergh was working in Russia. As Henry rode in a carriage, he witnessed a horse pulling another carriage fall to the ground. He was shocked when the driver began beating the fallen horse. Henry realized that working animals everywhere had no legal protection and he was determined to do something about it.

Henry Bergh quit his job and returned to New York, where he established the American Society for the Prevention of Cruelty to Animals (ASPCA). This organization immediately began to help. In 1867, for example, it operated the first ambulance for injured horses. This was two years before there were ambulance services for humans.

The ASPCA has supported the protection of millions of animals throughout the years. And now, there are thousands of animal shelter and rescue organizations across the United States.

ADOPTING AN ANIMAL

When you adopt an animal, you are adding a new member to your family. It is important to consider many things before you start your search:

- What type of animal is best for you and your family? Research the animal you are thinking of adopting. Find out all you can about its traits, feeding, and care.

- What are the costs of adopting an animal? There are adoption fees as well as licensing, medical care, food, and supplies.

- All animals require time and attention. Will you be available to be a companion and provide proper care?

- Animals require space—some more than others. Does your home have what is needed for the type of animal you want?

- How would your family benefit from adopting a pet?

- An animal should be welcomed as a member of a family. How do others in your home feel about adopting an animal?

- Does anyone have any allergies? Any fears? Any objections?

- Does your family already have other animals? How would a new animal get along with them?

- What community organizations can help you and your adopted animal? There are 4-H groups in both farm and city communities that offer many resources for raising and showing animals. Specific breed organizations may offer regular meetings and advice.

FAMILY SUPPORT IN ANIMAL ADOPTION

Just wanting a pet is not a good reason to get one. In fact, it may be the one reason why so many animals end up in animal shelters. But let's start with you wanting to adopt a pet. Now try this:

1. Write a letter *to yourself* about adopting a pet. Why do you think you would be a good companion and pet owner? How will you and your family benefit from having this animal? What can you contribute in terms of cost and care? How will adopting a pet be a great thing? Will you get lots of exercise walking it? Will you learn about caring for others?

2. After reading your letter, if you think you would be a good pet owner, write *a second letter to your family*. Share your research. Show your family that you are serious and really committed. It won't hurt to mention that you know that all pets poop and you are willing to clean up after your pet!

CAN'T ADOPT BUT WOULD LIKE TO HELP?

Not everyone can adopt an animal, but there are still lots of ways you can help support animals that need a home. You can check your local animal shelters, veterinary clinics, pet shops, and feedstores for opportunities to be involved with animals that will be grateful for your time. If you belong to a local service troop or organization, check with your leader for projects that support local animal shelters. Check bulletin boards or ask an adult to help you do website searches for local shelter and rescue organizations. Look for activities such as:

- Fostering animals awaiting adoption
- Participating in guide- or companion-dog training programs
- Walking dogs at local shelters
- Reading to animals in shelter care
- Fundraising for animal rescue, shelter, and placement organizations

The poems in *Tails from the Animal Shelter* wiggled, hopped, and flew into the author's hands. But nonfiction passages came from exploring lots of reading about various animals, shelters, and rescue missions. Readers, teachers, librarians, and families might also like to read some of the many sources which informed the author.

RESOURCES

Adopt a Pet
www.adoptapet.com

American Humane
www.americanhumane.org

American Society for the Prevention of Cruelty to Animals (ASPCA)
www.aspca.org

Animal Sheltering, in partnership with the Humane Society of the United States
www.animalsheltering.org
www.humanesociety.org

Best Friends
bestfriends.org

PETA
www.peta.org

PETA Kids
www.petakids.com

The Shelter Pet Project
theshelterpetproject.org